# A Visitor

# Matlock

## by John N. Merrill

Maps, photographs and sketches by John N. Merrill

*"I hike the footpaths and trails of the world for others to enjoy."*

# 2003

## The Peak District
## Visitor's Guides Series

## Walk & Write Ltd.

# Walk & Write Ltd.,
## Marathon House,
## Longcliffe, Nr. Matlock,
## Derbyshire, England. DE4 4HN

### Tel/Fax 01629 - 540991
### email - marathonhiker@aol.com

International Copyright John N. Merrill & Walk & Write Ltd. All rights reserved. No part of this publication may be reproduced or transmitted in any form or by any means electronic or mechanical including photocopy, recording or any information storage or retrieval system in any place, in any country without the prior written permission of Walk & Write Ltd.

John N. Merrill asserts his moral right to be identified as the authors of this work with the Copyright, Designs and Patents Act, 1988.

Typset and designed by John N. Merrill & Walk & Write Ltd.
Printed and handmade by John N. Merrill.

©
© Text - - John N. Merrill. 2003.
   Photographs, Maps & sketches - John N. Merrill. 2003.

ISBN 1-874754-27-6
First published January 1994 - . Revised and reprinted - May 2003

British Library Cataloguing-in-Publication Data. A catalogue record of this book is available from the British Library.

Typeset in Times bold, italic, and plain 11pt, 14pt and 18pt .

Please note - The maps in this guide are purely illustrative. You are encouraged to use the appropriate 1:25,000 O.S. map.

John Merrill has walked all the routes in this book. Meticulous research has been undertaken to ensure that this publication is highly accurate at the time of going to press. The publishers, however, cannot be held responsible for alterations, errors, omissions, or for changes in details given. They would welcome information to help keep the book up to date.

Cover design - by John N. Merrill - Walk & Write Ltd 2003.
Cover photograph - by John N. Merrill.

# A little about John N. Merrill

Few people have walked the earth's crust more than John Merrill with more than 178,000 miles in the last 32 years - the average person walks 75,000 miles in a lifetime. Apart from walking too much causing bones in his feet to snap, like metal fatigue, he has never suffered from any back, hip or knee problems. Like other walkers he has suffered from many blisters, his record is 23 on both feet! He wears out at least three pairs of boots a year and his major walking has cost over £125,000. This includes 95 pairs of boots costing more than £11,600 and over £1,800 on socks - a pair of socks last three weeks and are not washed!

His marathon walks in Britain include - -

Hebridean Journey....... 1,003 miles. Northern Isles Journey......913 miles.
Irish Island Journey .......1,578 miles.     Parkland Journey.......2,043 miles.
Land's End to John o' Groats.....1,608 miles.
The East of England Heritage Route - 450miles.

and in 1978 he became the first person to walk the entire coastline of Britain - 6,824 miles in ten months.

In Europe he has walked across Austria - 712 miles - hiked the Tour of Mont Blanc, the Normandy coast, the Loire Valley (450 miles), a high level route across the Augverne(230 miles) and the River Seine (200 miles) in France, completed High Level Routes in the Dolomites and Italian Alps, and the GR20 route across Corsica in training! Climbed the Tatra Mountains ,the Transylvanian Alps in Romania, and in Germany walked in the Taunus, Rhine, the Black Forest (Clock Carriers Way) and King Ludwig Way (Bavaria). He has walked across Europe - 2,806 miles in 107 days - crossing seven countries, the Swiss and French Alps and the complete Pyrennean chain - the hardest and longest mountain walk in Europe, with more than 600,000 feet of ascent! In 1998 he walked 1,100 miles along the pilgrimage route from Le Puy (France) to Santiago (Spain) and onto Cape Finisterre; in 2002 walked 700 miles from Seville to Santiago de Compostela.

In America he used The Appalachian Trail - 2,200 miles - as a training walk, before walking from Mexico to Canada via the Pacific Crest Trail in record time - 118 days for 2,700 miles. Recently he walked most of the Continental Divide Trail and much of New Mexico; his second home. In 1999 he walked the Chesopeake & Ohio Canal National Historical Trail. In 2,000 he became the first thru hiker to walk 1,340 miles around Ohio, following the Buckeye Trail. In Canada he has walked the Rideau Trail - Kingston to Ottowa - 220 miles and The Bruce Trail - Tobermory to Niagara Falls - 460 miles.

In 1984 John set off from Virginia Beach on the Atlantic coast, and walked 4,226 miles without a rest day, across the width of America to Santa Cruz and San Francisco on the Pacific coast. This is one of the finest and most memorable walks, being in modern history, the longest, hardest crossing of the U.S.A. in the shortest time - under six months (178 days). The direct distance is 2,800 miles.

Between major walks John is out training in his own area - The Peak District National Park. He has walked all of our National Trails many times - The Cleveland Way thirteen times and The Pennine Way four times in a year! He has been trekking in the Himalayas five times. He created more than thirty-five challenge walks which have been used to raise more than £600,000 for charity. From his own walks he has raised over £100,000. He is author of more than 225 walking guides which he prints and publishes himself, His book sales are in excess of 3 million, He has created many long distance walks including The Limey Way, The Peakland Way, Dark Peak Challenge walk, Rivers' Way, The Belvoir Witches Challenge Walk, The Forest of Bowland Challenge. the Dore to New Mills Challenge Walk , the Lincolnshire Wolds "Black Death" Challenge Walk and the Happy Hiker (White Peak) Challenge Walk. His new Pilgrim Walk Series includes the 72 mile, "Walsingham Way" - Ely to Walsingham. His monthly walks appear in Derbyshire's "Reflections" magazine. In January 2003, he was honoured for his walking and writing, recieving a Honorary degree, Master of the University, from Derby University.

# Contents

# INTRODUCTION

*Here in wild pomp, magnificently bleak,*
*Stupendous Matlock towers amid the Peak;*
*Here rocks on rocks on forests forests rise,*
*Spurn the low earth, and mingle with the skies,*
*Great Nature, slumbering by fair Derwent's stream,*
*Conceived these giant-mountains in a dream.*
James Montgomery

Visiting Matlock and Matlock Bath one finds it hard to believe that such a scenically attractive place should only have been a tourist centre for about the last 160 years. Matlock Dale with its tall limestone buttresses and flowing river Derwent is a place of dramatic beauty. Until the coming of the Spa era last century there was no road through the dale, and the route to Matlock was over Starkholmes, to the west. With the development of the Spa, the place became very popular. Many of the notable people of the day visited the area and walked in the dale, climbed the heights and took the waters. By the early part of this century such heady days were becoming a piece of history, as the popularity of the hydropathy establishments waned.

Despite this, and because of its scenic qualities, the area remains an increasingly popular place to explore. On the town's doorstep is the Peak District National Park and *"Peak Practice"* country whose beauty and differing characteristics are a never ending pleasure. These two attributes combined make the Matlocks a splendid base in which to linger a few days and enjoy a fascinating area of central England.

*Happy exploring!*
*John N. Merrill*

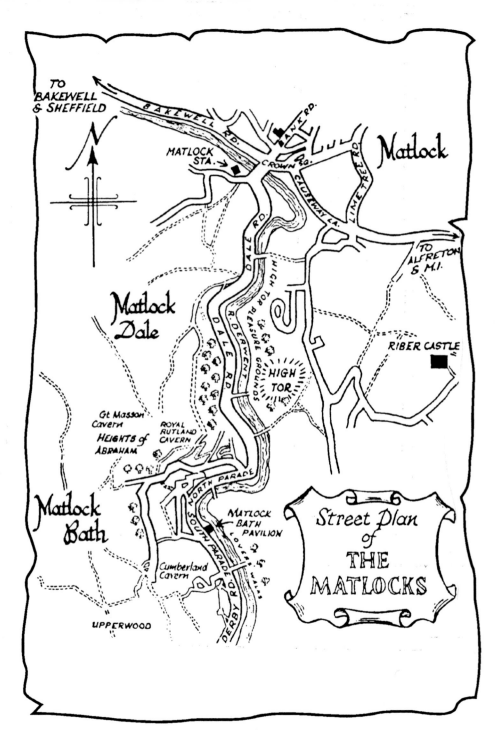

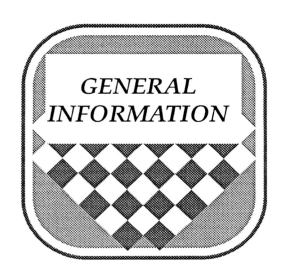

# GENERAL INFORMATION

Matlock is in Derbyshire and lies centrally within the county. The town is the largest within the area of the Derbyshire Dales District Council and is where the Derbyshire County Council has its administrative offices. The Peak District National Park lies to the south and west of the town. Matlock is 145 miles from London, 48 miles from Manchester, 22 miles from Sheffield, 25 miles from Nottingham, 18 miles from Derby, 10 miles from Chesterfield and 8 miles from Bakewell. The main A6 road runs through the town giving easy access from the north and south. The A632 Chesterfield road gives access from the nearby Ml motorway. Eastwards is the A615 road to Alfreton. There are daily bus services from the neighbouring towns and cities. A pay train from Derby operates daily via Cromford and Matlock Bath stations to Matlock.

**Population:** 20,320.
**Area of Parish District:** 16,598 acres.
**Early Closing Day:** Thursday.

**Shops:**
**Matlock** - Causeway Lane, Crown Square, Dale Road, Firs Parade and Smedley Street.
**Matlock Bath** - North and South Parade.

**Market Days:** Tuesday and Friday. Market beside the Central Bus Station.

**Ordnance Survey map showing Matlock and its surrounding area:**

1:50,000 Series. Sheet No. 119—"Buxton, Matlock and Dovedale".

1:25,000 Pathfinder Series Sheet No. SK 25/35 - Matlock (South).

1:25,000 Outdoor Leisure Map - The White Peak - east sheet.

**Rainfall:** Yearly average 40 inches.

 an average of 700 hours of sunshine during June, July and August.

 **Matlock** - Bakewell Road, Station Road, Old English Road, Bank Road.

**Matlock Dale** - Artists' Corner; **Matlock Bath** - The Pavilion, Royal Hotel Grounds, Railway Station.

 **Matlock** - Bakewell Road, Hall Leys Park.

**Matlock Dale** - Artists' Corner. **Matlock Bath** - North Parade, South Parade.

**📞Kiosks -** Matlock - Bank Road. Matlock Green, Matlock Bridge .Matlock Dale, Artists' Corner. Matlock Bath—North Parade, South Parade.

**ℹ️** The Central Library, The Firs, Steep Turn pike, Matlock, displays notices for forthcoming events. For Peak District National Park see Information Centre, Old Market Hall Bakewell; tel. Bakewell 01629 - 813227. The Peak Park Planning Board publishes annually, *"The Peakland Post"* with a calendar of events.

**Information Office:** Pavilion Gardens, Matlock Bath; tel. Matlock (01629) - 55082

**Police Station:** Matlock Bank Road; tel. Matlock 01629 - 580100.

**🚆** Matlock, Matlock Bath, Cromford. Daily Pay Train to and from Derby. Train enquiries, Tel. Derby 01332 - 32051.

**Public Library:**
Main Library, The Firs, Steep Turnpike, Matlock; tel. Matlock 01629 - 582480.
Branch Library, Whitworth Institute, Darley Dale.

♻National Westminster Bank Ltd., at Matlock and Matlock Bank.
Matlock - Midland Bank Ltd., ✖Royal Bank of Scotland, TSB.
**Building Societies** - Matlock - Derbyshire Building Society. Britannia Building Society. Halifax Building Society.

Church of England—St. Giles, Matlock; All Saints', Matlock Bank, St. John's, Matlock Dale, Holy Trinity, Matlock Bath. Roman Catholic—St. Joseph's Bank Road, Matlock. Methodist Church—Trinity, Bank Road, Matlock; Starkholmes; Matlock Moor. Congregational—Chesterfield Road, Matlock.

**Caravan Sites**: Darwin Forest Country Park, Darley Moor, Two Dales. Tel. 01629-732428. W. H. George, Alderwasley Park, Whatstandwell; tel. Ambergate 852063. Mrs. W. Millward, Miners Standard, Winster; tel. Winster 650279.

**Camping Sites**: W. H. George, Alderwasley Park, Whatstandwell; tel. Ambergate 852063.

**Youth Hostel**: 40, Bank Road, Matlock. tel. Matlock 01629 - 582983.

Bus and Coach Services: All buses leave the main Bus Station, Bakewell Road, Matlock, and operate a daily service. Current time tables are on display.

**Local Newspapers**: Matlock Mercury (Weekly),Friday. Derbyshire Times (Weekly), Friday. Matlock Express (Weekly). Derby Evening Telegraph (Daily).

**Golf**: Matlock Golf Club, Chesterfield Road, Matlock; tel. Matlock 582191.

**Cricket**: Matlock Cricket Club plays on Causeway Lane Sports Ground. Darley Dale Cricket Club plays on ground near Darley Bridge.

**Football**: Matlock Town Football Club, Causeway Lane, Matlock.

**Tennis:** Public hard courts in Hall Ley's Park, Matlock.

**Bowls:** Green in Hall Ley's Park, Matlock.

**Swimming:** Public Pool - The Lido, Bank Road, Matlock. Tel. 01629 - 582843.

**Children's Playground:** Hall Ley's Park - boating, paddling pool, swings. miniature railway.
Derwent Gardens, Matlock Bath - amusement ground and miniature railway.

**Boating:** On river Derwent from Matlock Bath.

**Fishing:** Trout and coarse fishing Matlock and Matlock Bath area—The Matlock Angling Club, Cromford—The Cromford Fly Fishing Club.

**Gardens:** Hall Ley's Park, Matlock. High Tor Pleasure grounds, Matlock Bath; Riverside Gardens, Matlock Bath; Derwent Gardens, Matlock Bath.

**Petrifying Wells:** Matlock Bath.

**Aquarium,** - Matlock Bath. Open daily.

**Entertainment:** Grand Pavilion, Matlock Bath. Dances and entertainment—in July the Miss Derbyshire contest is held here.

**Illuminations:** Matlock Bath, from mid August to mid October. Venetian Night, Saturday. Fireworks displays, decorated boats and band concerts.

**Weathercall** - 5 day forecast. Tel. 0891 - 505312.

# Where to stay

**Packhorse Farm, Tansley, Matlock, Derbys. DE4 5LF**
Modernised farmhouse set in lovely gardens. Quiet location, yet only 3 miles outside Matlock in elevated south facing position with extensive views. Log fires, full English breakfast and tea/coffee making facilities, colour TV in rooms. Open all year. Tel. 01629 - 580950 Byron and Susan Haynes,

*Dimple House, Dimple Road, Matlock, DE4 3JX*
*19th century private house, close to centre of Matlock. Large garden,*
*sitting room, conservatory. Comfortable rooms and a warm welcome.*
*Ideal base for exploring the beautiful Peak District.*
*Open - March-November. Mrs G. Parkinson. Tel. 01629 - 583228*

**MATLOCK AREA** - Several cottages - selection of sizes sleeping 2 - 15.
Panoramic views over Derwent valley. Shops, pubs & restaurants nearby.
Contact - Mr. P.M.Kelman, 8, Linbery Close, Oakerthorpe,
Derbyshire. DE5 7NT. Tel. 01773 - 833007. Fax. 01773 - 742276

**GREENBANK - Bed & Breakfast - Matlock Bath.**
**Tel. 01629 - 583909**
**Victorian Private house in quiet location overlook-**
**ing gorge. All rooms H & C with T.V's, tea & coffee**
**facilities. £15p.p. Non smoking.**

Holiday cottage in beautiful wooded Matlock Dale, opposite High Tor. Adjoins owners' Victorian House in large
garden. 2 bedrooms, G.C.H., private parking, no pets and
no smoking.
*For details telephone Peter or Anna Reed - 01629 - 583878*

**BRADVILLA - MATLOCK** - Private Victorian house, pleasant
views, comfortable, very friendly atmosphere, good food, central
heating Off the road parking. T.V. tea/coffee. Open all year except
Xmas.One double with own bathroom and sitting room and one
double/family or twin. B.& B. p.p. - £15 - £16.50. Mrs Jean Saunders,
26, Chesterfield Road, Matlock. Tel. 01629 - 57147

Quality en-suite accomodation in unique converted chapel.
Extensive views of Derbyshire countryside. Full English
or Vegetarian breakfast and evening meals.
Enquiries to Fay Whitehead - Tel. 01773 - 857008
Mount Tabor House, Bowns Hill, Crich. Derbyshire.

11

# Where to eat

**THE WHEATSHEAF** St. John's Street, Wirksworth.
*Tel. 01629 - 825299*
Harry & Maureen welcome all customers old and new.
*Specialising in Traditional Sunday lunches.*
We are now taking bookings for the new function room.

**THE BOAT INN, Scarthin, Cromford**
This olde world 18th century inn, with its cosy open fires, candle-light and stone surroundings provide a perdect setting to enjoy our "unusual" and reknowned menu. Voted Camra *"Pub of the Month"* - August 1995. Meals served daily - lunch and evening.
Open for morning coffee. Telephone 01629 - 823282.

**WELLINGTON FISH BAR - (Mary & Ernie Essex)**
**26, Wellington Street, Matlock. Tel. 01629 - 584141**
**We use only Best Quality Products. Open -**

| | | |
|---|---|---|
| *Tues - 11.45 - 1.30* | *5 - 10.30* | *Wed - 11.45 - 1.30  closed* |
| *Thurs - 11.45 - 1.30* | *5 - 10.30* | *Fri - 11.30 - 1.30  5 - 10.30* |
| | *Sat - 11.45 - 1.30  5 - 10.30* | |

**PROMENADE FISH BAR**
Best quality food, fresh fish daily,
with restaurant attached. Prime spot in Matlock Bath.
128 - 130, North Parade. Tel. 01629 - 584662

Tuckers Fish & Chips
**HIGH QUAILTY FISH & CHIPS**
18, North Parade, Matlock Bath.
Tel. 01629 - 57306

# WHITE
# LION
# INN

**Starkholmes,**
**Matlock.**
**Tel. 01629 - 582511**
* Bed & Breakfast
* Lunchtime & Evening meals
* Traditional Beers
* Boules Pitch
* Parties catered for

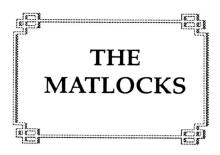

# THE MATLOCKS

When dealing with the history and development of Matlock one soon realises, after studying a map, that the area was originally a cluster of small hamlets. Their names are still used today—Matlock Bank, Matlock Bridge, Matlock Green, Matlock Town, Matlock Dale and Matlock Bath. The name Matlock means - *"Oak where the meetings were held."* It wasn't until the discovery of the medicinal springs in Matlock Bath at the end of the 17th century that the story of the town really begins. Even so, it was slow in developing and did not gather momentum until the 19th century when it mushroomed out during the spa era. As a result one should not simply talk about Matlock but rather the Matlocks. The rise and fall of hydropathy here has left its mark, as well as memories of the cable tramway up Bank Road and other fascinating features of past days. A wander around will bring you to sites and buildings of the spa era, many of which are used for other purposes today.

THE MATLOCK SPA ERA

Matlock Bath did not become a major spa until the 19th century. In fact its history is short, beginning in 1698 when the first spring was discovered—the Old Bath. Access to the spring was almost nil, but four years later in 1702 a coach road was made to Matlock Bath as it became known. In 1735 another spring was found, a quarter of a mile from the original, and later a third was found in Museum Parade. Daniel Defoe in his *"A Tour thro' the Island of Great Britain"* (1724-6) noted that at Matlock Bath there was *"a house built over it, and room within the building to walk round the bath, and so go by steps down gradually into it. The water is but just milk warm, so that it is less pleasant to go into than sanative."* The temperature varied between 68° and 72° degrees Fahrenheit.

By the beginning of the 19th century there were four springs and the hotels were described as having "very good accommodation". In 1802 the cost of hiring a bedroom was 5 shillings (25p) for a week and a private parlour one guinea(£1.05), Breakfast was 15 pence (6p), dinner two shillings (10p) and supper one shilling (5p). A medicinal bath cost six pence (2 1/2p). In 1815 the newly improved roads were giving greater access, and by 1838 Matlock Bath was a fashionable spa with regular coach traffic. Many of the leading personalities of the day, such as Lord Byron and Ruskin, made several visits. The thermal springs were described as being -

*"weak medicinal waters efficacious in colic, consumption, gout, chronic rheumatism, and cutaneous cases."*
*"when drunk freely it has proved beneficial in dyspeptic and rephritic cases."*
*"To its daily consumption many of the old inhabitants ascribe their good health and longevity."*

The success of the spa was assured. With easy access, the stunning countryside of the River Derwent, the limestone bastions of High Tor and pleasant walks, it soon became a popular place and has remained so ever since, although the springs have not been used for years.

The *"father of the Matlock spa"* is John Smedley, born at Wirksworth on June 12th, 1803. His father owned a hosiery business which, in 1818, moved from Wirksworth to Lea Mills, where it still is today. His younger brother died in 1827 leaving his father heart-broken. As a result John Smedley took over the business and expanded its production, and in 1847 married Caroline Harward, the second daughter of the Rev. John Harward, Vicar of Wirksworth. While on their honeymoon, John Smedley caught a chill which later turned to a fever. He returned to England and went to Ben Rhydding, a hydropathic establishment in Yorkshire where the cure was a complete success.

From this moment onwards he became so involved with hydropathy that he sold his business and in 1853 opened his first hydro. Until then, Matlock Bank was "a quiet hamlet of the old parish of Matlock, in which a few frame work knitters, cotton mill hands, agricultural labourers, and others, obtained a livelihood". In the late 1850s he began building his largest hydro here, and in time there were nine such establishments on the bank. John Smedley made a large fortune and built for himself Riber Castle, which was to his own design and cost £60,000. When he died in 1874 at the age of 71 he left behind his castle and hydro as two notable landmarks of Matlock. The castle became a school until 1929, after which it was left to decay until a group of zoologists purchased it in 1962. Today its grounds house one of the most comprehensive collections of British and European wild life in the country. His hydro served as a hospital during the first World War. During the second World War it was used by the army and in 1955 was purchased by Derbyshire County Council to form the administrative centre of the county.

16

# MATLOCK CABLE TRAMWAY

Running from Crown Square up Bank Road to the top of Rutland Street was a cable tramway which linked the hydros with the town. In its half mile length it climbed 300 feet, making it the steepest tramway in the world, with a gradient of 1 in 5 1/2. The main driving force in the project was Sir George Newnes, who was born at Matlock Bath and was the publisher of *"Tit Bits"* and the *"Strand Magazine"*. With several local people he was responsible for providing the finance for the tramway, which was officially opened on March 28th, 1893, and ceased operating 34 years later on September 30th, 1927. The fare was *"tuppence up the bank"* and 1d. down.

There were three trams, one being held in reserve. Working on a cable and pulley system the two trams in use moved up and down the line in unison with the passing place at Smedley Street, which today is still wider than Bank Road. At the top of Rutland Street on the left-hand side are the buildings of the depot which cost £2,600. The trams were royal blue and white in colour and the seats were of the garden seat variety with reversible backs. There was room for 13 passengers inside and 18 outside. Each tram travelled at a maximum speed of 5 1/2 miles per hour and if necessary could be stopped dead within its own length. The braking system was cleverly worked out and not once did it fail to operate. On Good Friday each year, the start of the tourist season, the drivers were issued with new uniforms.

In 1898 Sir George Newnes bought out his fellow shareholders for some £20,000 and presented the tramway to Matlock Council. Throughout its life it was never a financial success and after twenty years of operation to 1913 had lost £800. During the next fourteen years the tramway was losing an average of £1,000 per year; at the time of its closure in 1927 the accumulated loss was over £30,000.

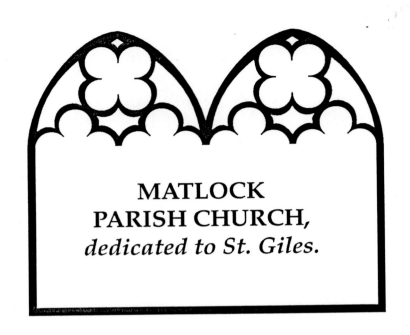

# MATLOCK PARISH CHURCH,
## *dedicated to St. Giles.*

The church dates back to Norman times, although little remains of this earlier building except some fragments outside the tower. The present building has a 15th century tower with the remainder being 19th century. Before venturing inside it is well worth while having a look at the 17th and 18th century gravestones, on which there are many interesting epitaphs. On the western side of the churchyard can be seen the tomb to Phoebe Brown (see folklore).

As you enter the nave the Woolley tomb is on your left. Anthony Woolley, who died in 1578 aged 72, owned Riber Hall which is now a restaurant. The style of clothes which both he and his wife are depicted as wearing was a short lived fashion. Above this altar tomb is a black marble slab to Adam Woolley, who died in 1657 aged 100, and his wife, Grace, who died in 1669 at the age of 110. They were married for a total of 76 years. In the left-hand corner from these two tombs is a glass case containing five Cransties or funeral garlands. This is the largest single collection of such garlands in Derbyshire and one of the finest in the country. (See folklore section for further details of this 18th century custom).

The hexagonal font is about 750 years old and for a long while was simply abandoned and lay in the rectory gardens until in 1924 it was returned to its rightful place. In the tower archway is an 18th century painted board which records that Hayward was the chief benefactor of the gallery—it refers to the north gallery and was moved to its present position in 1871. The tower contains eight bells, one of which is pre-Reformation and bears the rare fylfot cross. On the left-hand side of the chancel arch is the Guild Chapel, the only modern one in existence. All the furnishings were given by local industries and the altar is made from Hopton stone. Among the carvings in the chancel can be seen one of St. Giles with his pet hind, which he is said to have rescued from a huntsman. Little is known about him but he lived in Southern France in the 8th century. The colourful east window is one of the most modern in Derbyshire; it was fitted in 1969 and designed by Lawrence Lee.

THE PARISH CHURCH OF
ST. GILES, MATLOCK

# Matlock Town Walk - 3 miles

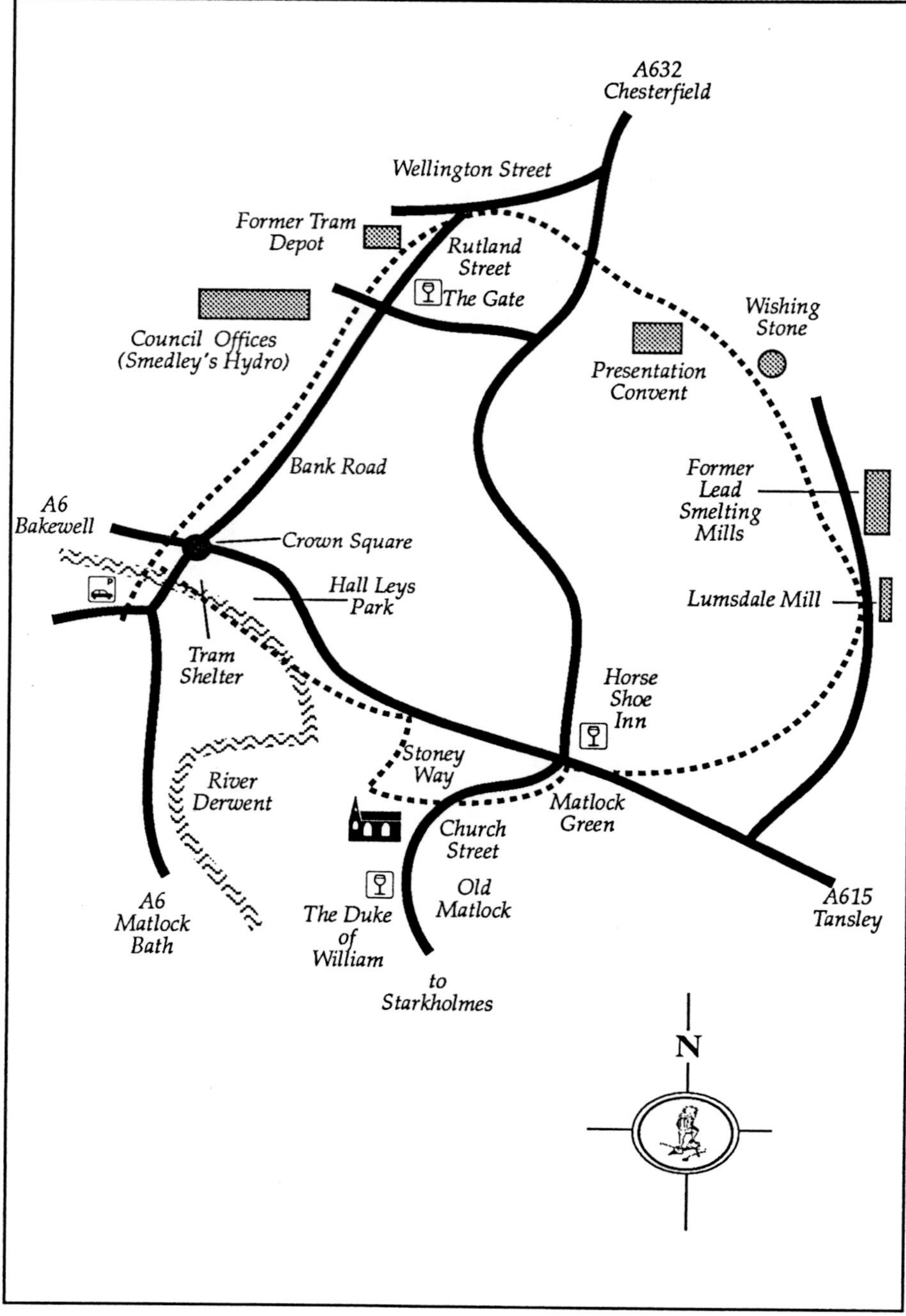

A632
Chesterfield

Wellington Street

Former Tram
Depot

Rutland
Street
The Gate

Wishing
Stone

Council Offices
(Smedley's Hydro)

Presentation
Convent

Bank Road

Former
Lead
Smelting
Mills

A6
Bakewell

Crown Square

Lumsdale Mill

Hall Leys
Park

Tram
Shelter

Horse
Shoe
Inn

Stoney
Way

River
Derwent

Matlock
Green

Church
Street

A615
Tansley

A6
Matlock
Bath

The Duke
of
William

Old
Matlock

to
Starkholmes

N

# A walk around Matlock - 3 miles - allow 2 hours.

••• ••• ••• ••• - *Car Park - Bank Road - Rutland Street - Wishing Stone - Lumsdale - Matlock Green - Parish Church - Hall Leys Park - Car Park.*

 *1:25,000 Outdoor Leisure Map - The White Peak - East Sheet.*

 *- Beside the Matlock Railway Station.*

*The Gate Inn, Rutland Street, Matlock. Horse Shoe Inn, Matlock Green. The Duke of William Inn, Old Matlock.*

ABOUT THE WALK - This short walk brings you to many of the places associated with the "Matlock" story. You get the hardest part over first by ascending Bank Road, following the line of the Matlock Cable Tramway. As you ascend you see the County Council offices, formerly Smedley's Hydro. From the old tram depot it is basically all down hill! First you cross to the wishing stone with views to Riber Castle and the Heights of Abraham. You descend steeply to Lumsdale and the remains of lead smelting. You pass several mills as you walk to Matlock Green and the short and gentle ascent to Old Matlock and the parish church. Here you descend for the last time to Hall Leys Park and return to the car park passing the iron tram shelter.

WALKING INSTRUCTIONS - From the car park turn left along the A6 over the River Derwent to Crown Square. Your route is straight ahead up Bank Road. Cross over to Bank Road and start ascending the road and line of the tramway. Pass the Post Office, Police Station, and Youth Hostel. Just beyond is the bulge in the road where the trams passed. Continue ascending to The Gate Inn. Continue ahead more steeply up Rutland Street to the road junction with Matlock Green Repair Garage on your left, in the former tram depot. Turn right, as footpath signed along a small road which soon becomes a tarmaced path. Follow this to the A632 - Chesterfield Road. Go straight across and follow a path to the road beside the Presentation Convent on your right. Follow the road which again becomes a tarmaced path and approaching houses keep left along the path to a road and houses. On your right is Bull Farm Mews. Turn right and in a few yards left and pass "Wishing Stone Cottage" on your right. Again this becomes a path and gain the large gritstone boulder, the wishing stone. Make your wish and just before the stone turn right and descend steeply

21

down the cobbled and stone stepped path. Keep descending to the road at Lumsdale. At the bottom it is worth turning left to explore the extensive buildings of the once very active lead smelting mills that date back to the mid 18th century.

Turn right and walk along the road passing Lumsdale Mill. 1/4 mile late reach another mill and turn right as footpath signed - Matlock and Hurst Farm. The path is mostly tarmaced and at the first path fork keep left. At the second fork, again keep left with playing fields on your right. Soon pass another mill on your left, as you follow a tarmaced path all the way to Matlock Green and the A615 road. Turn right along the road to Horse Shoe Inn. Here turn left along Church Street and ascend to St. Giles parish church. Just before it is Stoney Way, down which you descend. But first walk through the lynch gate and explore the church. Descend Stoney Way and turn left along the road and where it turns right keep straight ahead on the tarmaced "road" and walk through Hall Leys Park, passing the boating lake, band stand, tennis courts and tram shelter to reach Matlock Bridge and the A6. Turn left and retrace your steps back to the car park.

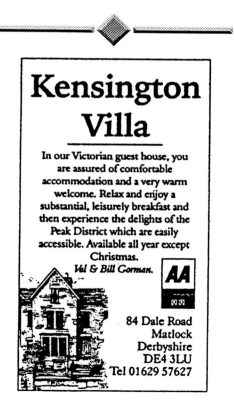

# THE HEIGHTS OF ABRAHAM

Matlock Bath is dominated by High Tor on its eastern side and the Heights of Abraham on the western side. Both are reached via footpaths and both are exceptional vantage points onto Matlock Bath and the river Derwent. The Heights of Abraham are so named because a soldier who had fought for General Wolfe in Quebec, Canada, in 1759 visited here and thought the hill was very similar to the Canadian one. The name has stuck ever since.

The grounds of the Heights of Abraham are gained via the entrance off Upperwood Road, Matlock Bath. There are numerous delightful wooded walks. Close to the summit and commanding a major vantage point is the Victoria Prospect Tower, built by John Petchell in 1844 when it provided work for local builders. Near to the tower is Great Masson Cavern and lower down through the grounds is the Great Rutland Cavern.

Built during the winter of 1983/4 and opened for Easter 1984 at a cost of £750,000, a cable car runs from a base station near the River Derwent, across the Derwent Valley to the summit, near the Heights of Abraham. The spectacular ride provides stunning views of the valley and High Tor.

Masson Hill is principally limestone laid down during the carboniferous era, 300 million years ago. Earth movements faulted the rock and formed channels, and along these flowed various ores—lead, copper and zinc. The main fault known as the Great Rake has been mined for lead since Roman times. During the 13th and 14th centuries there was a little mining, but it was from the 15th to the beginning of the 19th century that the industry became more intensive. When it ceased the mines were converted into show caves.

The first, Rutland Cavern, was opened to the public in 1810. Formerly it was known as Nestor Mine, but was named after the Duke of Rutland when a new entrance had been blasted through. There are 560 ft. of passageways to walk along as you visit the Roman Hall, Jacob's Wishing Well, Old Oak Tree and Nestor Grotto. Examples of pick work can be seen and many minerals and listen to a 16th century leadminer's story.

The Great Masson Cavern, opened in 1844, is principally an old lead mine with 2,000 ft. of passageways to walk along as you inspect a mine in use before explosives.

The caverns and Heights have frequently been visited by royalty. On July 25th, 1818, the Imperial Grand Duke Michael of Russia came and ascended the slopes on a pony. Princess Victoria and her mother, The Duchess of Kent, were here on October 22nd, 1832. In July 1840 the Dowager Queen Adelaide, widow of William IV, visited the grounds and was welcomed by a gun salute from the Heights.

Coffee shop. Tree Tops Visitor's Centre. Open from Easter to end of October. Tel. 01629 - 582365.

**WINGFIELD MANOR** (SK 375547): 8 miles south-east of Matlock. The manor, which is now a ruined shell, dates back to the mid 15th century. The public are allowed to wander around the ruins and see at first hand where Mary, Queen of Scots, was imprisoned. In the 16th century the manor belonged to the renowned Bess of Hardwick, Mary's guardian. On the site of Mary's apartments is a walnut tree, said to have grown from a nut dropped by Anthony Babington. During the Civil War the manor was occupied by both the Parliamentarians and Royalists and this largely accounts for the ruined state today. The banqueting hall and the crypt underneath are two notable places to visit. The seventy foot high tower is worth the ascent up the stone stairway for the summit gives an exceptional panorama of the ruins and of this area of Derbyshire.

**LEA HURST** (SK 325560): 4 miles S.W. This house was the home of the Nightingale family and of one of Britain's most famous women—Florence Nightingale. Her father was left Lea Hurst and in 1825 began altering the 17th century farm house to the present building. Over the main doorway can be seen "N 1825". Following the death of Florence the house remained in the family until Louis S. Nightingale died in 1940. It was then sold prior to auction and in 1951 was given to the Royal Surgical Aid Society. It has since been used as a home for the elderly: the house and gardens are open once a year to the public on the Saturday and Sunday of the second week in August.

**WINSTER MARKET HOUSE** (SK 242606): 5 miles N.W. Dominates the main street, standing almost in the middle of it. The building dates from the end of the 17th century and formerly had open arches. With the decline of markets and fairs in the 19th century it began to decay. In 1906 it was bought by the National Trust, who restored it, and was for a long time the only building owned by them in Derbyshire. Today, the Market House serves as a Trust information centre and shop and is open to the public on Wednesday, Saturday and Sunday afternoons during the summer months.

**HADDON HALL** (SK 235664): 7 miles N.W. The Hall dates back to the 12th century and spans 400 years of building with the long gallery being completed in the mid 16th century. It is the finest manorial home in England and a seat of the Duke of Rutland. During much of its building it was owned by the Vernon family; the last of the male line, Sir George Vernon, rests in Bakewell church. His daughter, Dorothy Vernon, brought the Hall into the Rutland family by marrying Sir John Manners. A love story is woven about these two; according to the tale she slipped out of the Hall at midnight and crossed the river Wye to meet Sir John. Together they rode into Leicestershire where they were married the next day. The building is full of interest with a chapel, banqueting room, kitchens, chambers and long gallery and there are many paintings and tapestries. The 400 year old walled gardens are a never-ending pleasure to walk through in June when the roses and clematis are in full bloom. The Hall and gardens are open to the public from Easter to the end of September - from 11-00 a.m. to 6-00 p.m. There are tea rooms and a car park opposite the entrance gates to the Hall. Tel. 01629 - 812855.

**CHATSWORTH HOUSE** (SK 260702): 8 1/2 miles N. One of the great houses of Europe and the home of the Dukes of Devonshire, who have played a major role in the history of Derbyshire. The present house dates from 1690 and was started by the first Duke. An Elizabethan house which stood on the same site, was built by Bess of Hardwick and was one of the places where Mary, Queen of Scots, was imprisoned. By the mid 19th century building work at Chatsworth was completed by the sixth Duke and his friend and head gardener, Sir Joseph Paxton. The house is rich in paintings, furniture, and Derbyshire treasures and needs several visits to appreciate the splendour of it all. The gardens, too, are both extensive and magnificent and also require repeated visits to see all they contain. The house and gardens are open to the public from Easter to the end of September, from 11-00 a.m. to 5-00 p.m. Tel. 01246 - 582204

**GULLIVER'S KINGDOM** - Matlock Bath. Theme park for families. Rides and attractions. Model village and minature world. Royal Cave tour. Open daily Easter to end of October; restricted Winter openings.Tel. 01629 - 580540.

**PEAK DISTRICT MINING MUSEUM & TEMPLE MINE** - Matlock Bath. The story of lead mining and experience what it was like to be a miner - crawl and climb through tunnels. Open all year. Tel. 01629 - 583834.

**HIGH TOR GROUNDS** - Matlock. 60 acres to explore with stunning views over Matlock Bath and River Derwent. The Tor is 396 feet above the river and the view is often referred to as *"The Switzerland View."* Small caves dating back to Roman times. Cafe. Open all year. Entrance charge.

**RED HOUSE STABLES - CARRIAGE MUSEUM** - Darley Dale. Over 40 horse-drawn vehicles, equipment and harness rooms. Tours and driving tuition can be arranged. Open throughout the year. Tel. 0629 - 733583.

**RIBER CASTLE** —Fauna Reserve and Wildlife Park: Looking down on Matlock from its perch 850 feet above sea level is the ruin of Riber Castle. Built last century, its grounds now house one of the largest collections of British and European animals and birds in the country. There is a large car park and picnic area beside the castle with the view of Matlock and the Derwent valley stretching before you. Among the many animals and birds to be seen are red fox, eagle owl, European Iynx, wild boar, fallow deer, reindeer, wild cats, storks, cranes, otters, polecats and pine martens. Open to the public every day. Tel. 01629 - 582073.

**NATIONAL STONE CENTRE**, nr. Wirksworth. *"Story of Stone"* exhibition. Trails to quarries to see 300 million year old fossil reefs and lagoons. Open all year. Tel. 01629 - 824833.

**HIGH PEAK JUNCTION WORKSHOPS** - Junction of High Peak Trail and Cromford Canal, near Cromford. Restored main room with forge, railway exhibition, shop and Information Centre. Open weekends and Bank Holidays - May to September.Tel. 01629 - 823204.

**CRICH TRAMWAY MUSEUM** - 6 miles S.E. On the outskirts of Crich village is this unusual but very absorbing museum of the "Tramway period." The collection of about fifty electric, horse-drawn and steam vintage trams, includes a wide range of both British and European trams, mostly built between 1873 - 1953. Many are in working order and trips can be taken down a mile of track on, for instance, Sheffield's last tram, on a Czechoslovakian tram, or on one from Blackpool. The museum is open from Easter to the end of October from 10-00 a.m. onwards. Tel. 01773 - 852565.

**PEAK RAILWAY LTD.** Steam trains run between Matlock and Darley Dale. Aim to reopen the line from Matlock to Buxton. Peak Railway shop, Matlock Station. Tel. 01629 - 580381.

# Industrial Archaeology

In 1771 Cromford was the scene of a major industrial revolution with the starting of Sir Richard Arkwright's water-powered cotton spinning mill, the first in the world. Cromford and its immediate area is extremely rich in industrial archaeology and is a fascinating place to explore. The following are some of the key places to visit.

**Cromford:** Sir Richard Arkwright's first cotton spinning mill is situated on the north-eastern side of the village, on the Starkholmes/Holloway road and is open to the public, managed by the Arkwright Society. Sir Richard, from 1771 onwards, went on to build numerous water-powered mills in Derbyshire. The most prominent one is Masson Mill just north of Cromford. In the space of 25 years he amassed a personal fortune of half a million pounds and through his work became known as the *"father of the factory system."* On the other side of the river Derwent can be seen Willersley Castle, which he built for himself, although he died before it was completed. The building is now used as a Methodist Conference Centre. A walk around Cromford village to see classic 18th century industrial housing will take an hour or two. The Greyhound Inn with its Georgian facade has not altered since Arkwright built it; behind it is the last of five mill ponds. It is possible to follow the stream from this pond, under the road, along a channel and finally over a cast iron lauder, dated 1821, into the Cromford Mill. By walking up the valley you will see the other four mill ponds.

Walking up the B5036 Wirksworth road, you will come to many 18th century houses built by Arkwright for his workers. The finest example is North Street, it is interesting to note the width of the street and the three-storey houses. Originally the third storey was one long continuous room where the occupants made stockings after working at the mill for twelve hours.

**Cromford Canal:** Running from Arkwright's first mill is the Cromford Canal. He was the main backer of the water way which was officially opened a year after his death, in 1793. The canal, 14 1/2 miles long, joins the Erewash Canal at Langley Mill and cost £80,000 to build. Finished goods and raw materials for the cotton mills were shipped on the canal, as was stone from the nearby quarries. There is a walk along the towpath to the High Peak Junction, wharf, Leawood Pump House and beyond. The waterway is currently being restored and the Derbyshire County Council has done considerable restoration work at different locations.

**High Peak Railway:** After surveying different alternative ideas it was decided to link together the Cromford Canal and the Peak Forest Canal at Whaley Bridge by rail. It was a most ambitious project because of the hilly nature of the ground. The line was 33 miles long from High Peak Junction, where the cargo was transshipped from canal barge to railway wagon. Josiah Jessop, whose father had designed the Cromford Canal, was the engineer of the line which was opened in 1830 and cost £180,000. The difficult terrain meant that originally there were nine steep inclines up which trains and wagons were winched. The first incline from High Peak Junction is known as Sheep Pasture. The line then goes under the Black Rocks of Cromford and on to the Middleton Incline — the engine house at the top has been preserved and the winding gear is still operational and is now a Visitor's Centre. By 1967 the line was closed, apart from at the Buxton end where it is still used by various limestone quarries. Part of the line, some 17 miles from High Peak Junction to Dowlow, near Buxton, has been converted into a footpath. The old railway stations have been removed and their sites are now car parks and picnic areas. From these it is possible to go along the High Peak Trail, passing through delightful countryside by ascending inclines, walking through cuttings, tunnels, and across embankments and seeing at first hand a remarkable industrial relic.

# Customs and Folklore.

Matlock and its surrounding area is a treasure trove of legends, traditions and customs. The following are just a few of them.

**Phoebe Brown:** Among the gravestones of St. Giles church is one to Phoebe Brown. Tombstones may not excite the imagination, but during the 19th century Phoebe was a local eccentric. She could break in horses—a major source of income for many years, she played the piano, could recite poems, and was a good markswoman. She never married and always dressed in male clothes. She is described as being "rough, rude, uncouth, eccentric, masculine, but she knew what was right and in her rough way abided by it". She died at the age of 84 in May 1854, and the curate of Matlock penned at the time:—

> *Here lies romantic Phoebe,*
> *Half Garymede, half hebe;*
> *A maid of notable condition,*
> *Jockey, cow herd and musician.*

**Funeral Garlands:** Just inside the parish church is a glass case on the left-hand side of the porch doorway. The case contains five garlands, often referred to as Cransties, which are believed to be 200 years old and are among the best surviving examples of this 18th-century custom. Others in Derbyshire to be seen are at Ashford-in-the-Water and South Trusley churches. When an unmarried female died before her marriage, a garland was made from thin wicker framework and covered with crepe paper and rosettes. Hanging down in the centre was either a paper handkerchief or glove and upon this was written the age, date and name of the person deceased. The garland was carried in front of the funeral procession and after the proceedings was hung above the deceased person's pew.

**The Wishing Stone:** Off the eastern side of Chesterfield Road (A632) at Matlock Bank is the footpath across Lumsdale. A short distance along it brings you to the wishing stone. According to tradition, you should sit on it and wish and your wish will come true!

**The Leap of B.H.:** On the eastern side of Cromford and near the drive to Willersley Castle is a road bridge across the river Derwent. At the southern end of it on the down stream parapet is a stone bearing the inscription:—*"The leap of R.M.B.H. Mare, June, 1697"*. How the stone came to be there appears to originate from the following story. Benjamin Hayward, who lived at Bridge House, Cromford, was riding along the road. On reaching the bridge his horse, instead of crossing it, suddenly leapt over the parapet, where the stone is today, and landed safely in the river. Despite the leap, Benjamin remained on horseback, crossed the river and climbed up the opposite bank to the road. Neither horse nor rider were injured as a result of their escapade.

**George Twyford:** He lived during the last century and was often nicknamed "*the wisest man in Matlock.*" He was basically a beggar and musician and would roam the streets during the tourist season, making himself a nuisance and trying to sing. Once he had been given a copper or two he left the people alone and sought out another likely group. He made sufficient money during the season to last him through the winter. The following story was often told about him. After going through his act for a couple of men they decided to give him a penny. One commented to the other that he wouldn't know the difference between a six pence and a penny, and so offered him both. Without hesitation George said: "*Ah wunna bi greydey' I'll tak' th' little 'un*". Pocketing the sixpence he walked away, leaving the men speechless!

*The Grand Pavilion,*
*Matlock Bath.*

# Walks - some suggestions -

Matlock and its surrounding area abounds with footpaths and walks of differing lengths. The Cromford Canal and the High Peak Trail with its car parks make ideal places for short walks. The following circular walks are a random selection in and around Matlock. The 1: 50,000 Series O.S. Map sheet No. 119 and 1:25,000 Pathfinder Series Sheet Nos SK 26/36 and SK 25/35 covers all of them. The walking instructions are simply guidelines and the Ordnance Survey sheet map is a must when walking any of these routes.

## From Matlock: *Route: Matlock - Riber - Dethick - Lea - Holloway - High Peak Junction - Cromford Canal - High Tor - Matlock. 8 miles.* From Matlock walk through Hall Ley's Park, past St. Giles church and Charles White School to ascend the hillside to Riber Castle. The view from the summit over Matlock is exceptional. From Riber follow the path across the fields to the road and Littlemoor Wood. A short road walk brings you to Dethick before paths to Lea and Holloway. From the latter village descend to near the river Derwent and follow the path which crosses the river and goes through the sewerage works to the Cromford Canal. Walk along the canal to Cromford Wharf before following the road to Starkholmes. Bear left and use the path over High Tor, with its spectacular view, before descending back to Matlock.

## Churchtown: *Route: Matlock - Darley Bridge - Churchtown - Two Dales - Upper Hackney - Matlock. 6 miles.* Half footpath and lane walking, but giving good views of the Derwent Valley north of Matlock. Follow footpath from the bridge over the River Derwent in central Matlock and keep along the left-hand bank of the river to Darley Bridge. Cross the river using the road before turning left and crossing the fields to St. Helen's church at Churchtown. By using the minor roads cross the A6 and continue into Darley Hillside and Two Dales village. At the latter follow the footpath to Upper Hackney where a final mile of road walking returns you to central Matlock from your elevated position.

## Bonsall: *Route: Matlock - Heights of Abraham - Bonsall - Brightgate - Tearsall Farm - Wensley Dale - Snitterton - Matlock. 7 miles.* The walk can be shortened considerably, either by omitting Wensley Dale and taking the path to Snitterton from Brightgate, or from Bonsall itself following the direct path to Matlock. From Matlock cross the river Derwent road bridge and walk up Snitterton Lane for a short distance before following the path via St. John the Baptist church to the Heights of Abraham. Maintain your height,— walking through woodland and later along a lane into Bonsall. Walk north through the village to Brightgate and the path to Tearsall Farm and Wensley Dale. Bear right out of the dale to Snitterton and a short walk returns you to Matlock.

See separate book - *"Short Circular Walks Around Matlock"* by John N. Merrill - for further walks & "Cycling Around Matlock" by A. Robinson.

**ASHOVER** (SK 348632): 4 miles N.E. A village of more than usual interest A board on the Crispin Inn recalls a day in 1646 when the Royalists threw the landlord out and drank his ale. Close by is the church which has many associations with the Babington family. The 128 ft. spire was built by them in the 15th century, and inside can be seen the tombs to members of the family. The most important treasure of the church is the lead font which dates from the 12th century. About 3/4 mile east of the village are the ruins of Eastwood Hall, which in the 17th century belonged to Immanuel Bourne. He was the rector and during the civil war tried to be neutral, but neither side trusted him and eventually the Parliamentarians blew up the Hall. On the southern fringe of the village is Overton Hall, the former home of Sir Joseph Banks. All these places and several others can be reached by the many footpaths and bridleways in the area.

**BIRCHOVER** (SK 240622): 5 miles N.W. A gritstone village surrounded by excellent walking areas. Stanton Moor is to the north and to the west is Cratcliffe Tor with its hermit's cave and Robin Hood's Stride. Close to the village are Stanton Quarries — the stone is a sandy pink colour and very durable and is used in the facing of many public buildings. At Upper Town on the southern perimeter of the village are the wooden stocks. On the western side of Birchover is the Druid Inn with Rowter Rocks behind; the rocks have passageways, steps and armchairs which were carved in them in the 18th century. There are also two rocking stones. At the chapel just down the lane from the Druid Inn is a plaque in the porch to Joan Waste who was burnt to death at the Windmill Pit, Derby on August 1st, 1555, for being a supposed heretic.

**BONSALL** (SK 280583): 3 miles S. Attractive limestone village and a former lead-mining community. In the centre and surrounded by 17th century buildings is the circular market cross with thirteen steps. The village observes the well-dressing custom in early August each year. The church is a noble building and dates back to the 13th century. Leading in all directions is a lattice work of footpaths through peaceful limestone countryside.

## DARLEY DALE (SK 275628): 3 miles N.E.

The actual town ship is made up of a group of villages—Two Dales, Darley Hillside, Churchtown and Darley Bridge. They are very interesting historically and the Darley Dale Society is responsible for a trail guide to many of the key places in the vicinity. Beside the A6 road is the Whitworth Hotel and Institute, named after Darley Dale's most famous person, Sir Joseph Whitworth. He was a prolific inventor and is best remembered for the Whitworth thread and rifle boring. He became immensely rich and lived at Stancliffe Hall, which is now a boys' preparatory school. Sir Joseph built the Institute which now houses a library and was a major local benefactor. St. Helen's church at Churchtown is an exceptional building. In the churchyard is a yew reputed to be 2,000 years old, and thus the oldest tree in Britain. The church itself contains many treasures and dates from Norman times. There is a monument to Sir John de Darley, who died in the 13th century and was a former lord of the manor and the Rollesley tombs are also worthy of note. There is much more to see and a visit to Darley Dale and its area makes a rewarding excursion.

## DETHICK (SK 328580): 3 miles S.E.

A very unusual village, being just a cluster of buildings close to the church. The village name, Dethick, means Death Oak. The church dates from the 13th century and is dedicated to St. John the Baptist. The tower was built in 1539 and part way up it are the heraldic shields of the Babington family who lived here. Their most famous member was Anthony Babington who was executed for being a leader of the Babington Plot to rescue Mary, Queen of Scots, from Wingfield Manor, five miles away. Footpaths lead you down into neighbouring villages of Lea and Holloway and to Riber Castle.

**LEA** (SK 327575): 3 miles S.E. Now immortailised by the ITV series - *"Peak Practice"* country. Small and attractive village between Dethick and Holloway. Several footpaths join all three villages together, while other paths lead one across pleasant countryside to Starkholmes, Matlock and Crich. On the southern fringe of Holloway is the former house of Florence Nightingale, Lea Hurst, which is open to the public on the second weekend in August. Nearby are the Lea Rhododendron Gardens—during late May and early June they are bursting into flower and colour and are open to the public daily.

**ROWSLEY** (SK 258658): 5 miles N. Although the A6 road goes through the centre of the village, there are several interesting historical buildings including Caudwell's flour mill - open to the public. One of the smallest surviving flour millers in the country and the machinery is driven by waterpower. In the village centre is the Peacock Hotel; over the porch can be seen the peacock which is part of the crest of the Manners family of nearby Haddon Hall. The building dates back to 1652 and was originally the private residence of John Stevenson, *"man of affairs"* to Grace, Lady Manners. On the southern outskirts of the village, the rivers Wye and Der went meet. Footpaths radiate from Rowsley enabling you to explore this region very fully.

**SNITTERTON** (SK 280604): 2 miles W. A small hamlet with one of the five bull rings of Derbyshire in the road—a stone slab on the roadside indicates its whereabouts. At the end of a "no through road" is Snitterton Hall, an Elizabethan Manor House believed to have been built by John Millward in 1631 and presently owned by the Bagshaw family. A variety of footpaths lead from the hamlet past the Hall onto Bonsall Moor, to Wensley and Wensley Dale, Oaker Hill, and to Matlock.

**WINSTER** (SK241606): 5 miles N.W. A limestone village of exceptional charm with the main street largely comprising of 18th century houses. The western end of the street is almost blocked by the 17th century Dower House, while the eastern end is dominated by the Market Hall, owned by the National Trust and open on Wednesday, Saturday and Sunday afternoons during the summer months. Between these two buildings the street is used for the annual pancake races on Shrove Tuesday, when the young and old run and toss pancakes. Set back from the main street is the imposing Hall around which the tale of a lover's leap is woven. Walking around the village and up both East and West Bank you come to many 18th century buildings of typical Derbyshire construction, with limestone walls and gritstone lintels and quoins.

**WIRKSWORTH** (SK 287539): 5 miles S. A limestone village rich in character and industrial archaeology, and a place that has much to offer the inquiring mind. Formerly it was an important lead-mining centre, and the barmaster and his jury still meet every six months at the 19th century Moot Hall. Plaques on either side of the main doorway illustrate the miners' craft. Wandering around the village you will find many tape works, which in the 19th century caused the term "red tape" to be coined. *"Adam Bede"*, the novel by George Eliot, is set in Wirksworth and its immediate area. At Whitsuntime the annual well-dressing ceremony takes place and the wells remain dressed for a week. The church with its small spire is a fascinating building dating back to Norman times—inside is a lead-lined font, the Wirksworth stone found near the altar last century and probably Saxon, and tombs to the Gell family who still live at Hopton Hall, two miles to the west. Just off the Market Place is Crown Yard with the Wirksworth Heritage Centre and Museum - well worth a visit.

*The Wirksworth Stone in the parish church - Anglo-Saxon sculpture.*